St. Paul's Nephew to the Rescue

Claudia Cangilla McAdam
Illustrated by Dave Hill

OSV kids
Huntington, Indiana

29 28 27 26 25 24 1 2 3 4 5 6 7 8 9

Our Sunday Visitor Publishing Division
Our Sunday Visitor, Inc.
200 Noll Plaza
Huntington, IN 46750
www.osv.com
1-800-348-2440

ISBN: 978-1-68192-984-2 (Inventory No. 2719)
1. JUVENILE NONFICTION—Religion—Bible Stories—General.
2. JUVENILE NONFICTION—Religious—Christian—General.
3. RELIGION—Christianity—Catholic.

LCCN: 2023938522

Cover and interior design: Lindsey Riesen
Cover and interior art: Dave Hill

PRINTED IN TURKEY

Dedication

With love for my grandson Joseph — may you always have the courage to do the right thing.
— CCM

The son of Paul's sister, however, heard about the ambush; so he went and entered the compound and reported it to Paul.
— Acts 23:16

Jonathan sped across Jerusalem's streets, clutching a bundle to his chest. His uncle Paul had been arrested! He needed the blanket and food Jonathan carried.

He ran down a narrow alleyway. A foot snaked out from behind a wall. Jonathan stumbled. A shove from behind sent him sprawling on the ground, scraping his arms.

Two boys towered over him. One was tall, and the other had mean eyes.

"What's the hurry?" the tall one asked.

The other boy grabbed at what Jonathan carried. Jonathan held it more tightly to his chest. His chin quivered slightly as he scrambled up.

The tall boy glared down at him. "Afraid?" he asked.

Jonathan was not brave, but he was fast.

By the time he reached the Roman fortress that held his uncle, Jonathan's elbows dripped with blood from his fall.

“What happened?” Paul asked.

“Some boys,” Jonathan answered.

“They don’t like you?”

Jonathan shook his head slowly. “I’m quiet. Small. Scared sometimes, and—” He glanced up to his uncle’s face.

Paul smiled. “And you are my nephew.”

Jonathan nodded.

"It is not easy for those who believe in Jesus," Paul said. "But we keep the Faith and run the race that is before us, so that one day we will receive a crown of victory. Five times I've been whipped with thirty-nine lashes. I've been beaten with rods three times. Once I was stoned."

Jonathan touched the scrapes on his arms. Compared to what his uncle had been through, they weren't that bad! He unwrapped the food and set it on a table as he listened.

His uncle continued. "Just today, when I was speaking before the council, the chief priest ordered someone to slap me," he said. His uncle turned his head. Jonathan could see the red handprint on his face and the cut along the edge of his mouth. "Christ will always be honored in my body, whether by life or by death."

Jonathan swallowed hard and held his skinned elbows. "How can you stand the pain?"

His uncle squeezed Jonathan's hand. "I can do all things through him who strengthens me. And so can you."

Jonathan wasn't so sure. He spread the blanket over his uncle's cot and sat down.

"Put on the armor of God so you can stand up against evil," Paul said. "God brings good out of even the worst things. Think of Our Lord's death. In everything, God works for good for those who love him. Always remember that."

The following day Jonathan searched the market for an ointment to apply to the bruise on Uncle Paul's face. He turned a corner and froze. A crowd huddled together. There must have been at least forty men in the group. Among them, he recognized the fathers of the two boys who had trapped him yesterday.

"So, are we agreed then?" one of the men said. "None of us will eat or drink anything until we have killed Paul!" The group cheered.

Jonathan quietly crept closer. He used his small size to hide.

The leader of the group pointed to another man. "You go to the officer who is holding Paul in the fortress," he said. "Tell him to bring the prisoner to the council tomorrow. Say that the elders want to hear Paul's case. When they bring Paul down that narrow passageway, we will be waiting to kill him."

Jonathan slipped away and sprinted to the fortress. He told Paul what he had heard. His uncle called to one of the soldiers.

"Bring this young man to the commander," he said. "He has something to tell him."

Jonathan trembled, but the commander took him gently by the hand. “What do you have to say to me?” he asked.

Jonathan told him about the plot to kill his uncle. The officer patted him on the shoulder. “Tell no one what you have told me,” he said.

He gave an order to two of his men. “Tonight, take two hundred soldiers, seventy men on horseback, and two hundred spearmen. Put Paul on a horse. Take him safely to the governor.”

Jonathan breathed in relief. His uncle would be safe.

Paul hugged Jonathan. "In everything, give thanks," he said. "Last night, the Lord appeared to me. He said, 'Take courage, for as you have spoken about me in Jerusalem, now you must also bear witness in Rome.' I didn't know how I could leave Jerusalem to do that, but your bravery has made it possible."

That night, Jonathan watched his uncle depart surrounded by soldiers. Paul sat on his horse, head high and back straight. Jonathan kept his eyes on his uncle until the blackness of the night swallowed him.

On his way home Jonathan hurried down the narrow alleyway. In the dim light he saw the tall boy and the one with mean eyes. Jonathan stopped, feeling his heart thudding in his chest. "In everything, give thanks," his uncle had said.

The two boys were bullying a younger boy and a little girl. Jonathan wanted to turn around and run. Instead, he closed his eyes and prayed. "Thank you for putting me here, Lord," he whispered. He straightened his back and held his head high.

Jonathan raced across the rough stones hollering, "Leave them alone!" The bigger boys whirled in his direction. He shouted to the younger children, "Run!"

"You!" the boys cried.

Jonathan skidded to a stop before he reached them and spun back the other way. The bullies chased after him, and the smaller children made their escape.

“In everything God works for good,” Jonathan thought. “I can do all things through him who strengthens me.”

He rounded a corner, picked up his pace, and using the night as his shield, disappeared into the darkness. This was a race he would not lose.

AUTHOR'S NOTE

St. Paul's Nephew to the Rescue is a tale based on a true story from the life of St. Paul as told in Acts of the Apostles 23:12–24.

While it is historical that Paul had a nephew, the hero of this story, we don't know his name or his age. It is believed that the nephew was a child at the time this incident took place, because Scripture tells us that "the commander took him by the hand" (Acts 23:19), something that someone might do with a child.

The facts we do know about the story are that St. Paul had come to Jerusalem to report to Christian leaders there about his missionary work to the Gentiles. Paul had enemies in Jerusalem who accused him of doing things he did not do. This upset many people and a riot began.

Paul was dragged out of the temple and was being beaten when a Roman officer came forth to try to settle matters. Because people were arguing about what Paul did and did not do, the soldier ordered Paul to be brought into the military compound to protect him from the violence of the mob.

That night, Jesus appeared to Paul and told him, "Take courage. For just as you have borne witness to my cause in Jerusalem, so you must also bear witness in Rome" (Acts 23:11).

The next day, some of the Jewish leaders plotted to kill Paul. Paul's nephew heard about the plan, and what he did with that knowledge is what I've written about in this book. Because of his nephew's daring actions, Paul was safely moved from Jerusalem at night, the first step that led to his being able to go to Rome and preach about Jesus.

May all of us be brave enough to proclaim the Lord Jesus Christ and to be willing to risk our lives for him and for others.

Claudia Cangilla McAdam

For a free Discussion and Activities Guide for this book, visit www.claudiamcadam.com.

Acts 23:12-24

12 When day came, the Jews made a plot and bound themselves by oath not to eat or drink until they had killed Paul.

13 There were more than forty who formed this conspiracy.

14 They went to the chief priests and elders and said, "We have bound ourselves by a solemn oath to taste nothing until we have killed Paul.

15 You, together with the Sanhedrin, must now make an official request to the commander to have him bring him down to you, as though you meant to investigate his case more thoroughly. We on our part are prepared to kill him before he arrives."

16 The son of Paul's sister, however, heard about the ambush; so he went and entered the compound and reported it to Paul.

17 Paul then called one of the centurions and requested, "Take this young man to the commander; he has something to report to him."

18 So he took him and brought him to the commander and explained, "The prisoner Paul called me and asked that I bring this young man to you; he has something to say to you."

19 The commander took him by the hand, drew him aside, and asked him privately, "What is it you have to report to me?"

20 He replied, "The Jews have conspired to ask you to bring Paul down to the Sanhedrin tomorrow, as though they meant to inquire about him more thoroughly,

21 but do not believe them. More than forty of them are lying in wait for him; they have bound themselves by oath not to eat or drink until they have killed him. They are now ready and only wait for your consent."

22 As the commander dismissed the young man he directed him, "Tell no one that you gave me this information."

23 Then he summoned two of the centurions and said, "Get two hundred soldiers ready to go to Caesarea by nine o'clock tonight, along with seventy horsemen and two hundred auxiliaries.

24 Provide mounts for Paul to ride and give him safe conduct to Felix the governor."

More Books from OSV Kids

In This Catholic Church
by Maura Roan McKeegan

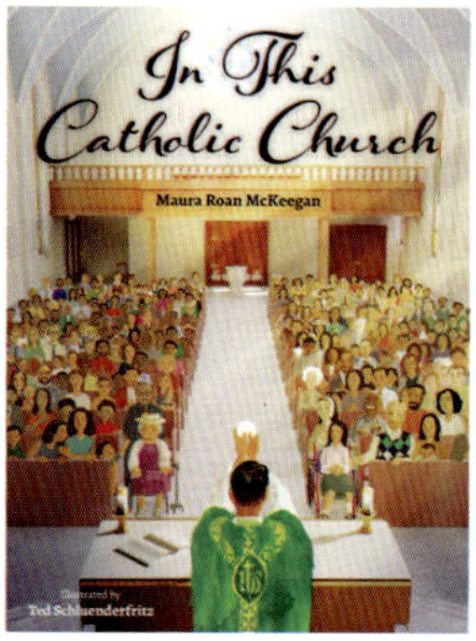

In This Catholic Church, a beautifully illustrated cumulative tale, celebrates our Church as a true family, from the people and families in the pews to the priest at the altar, and the love of Jesus Christ who abides in the hearts of his people.

Jesus and the Miracle of the Mass
by Gracie Jagla

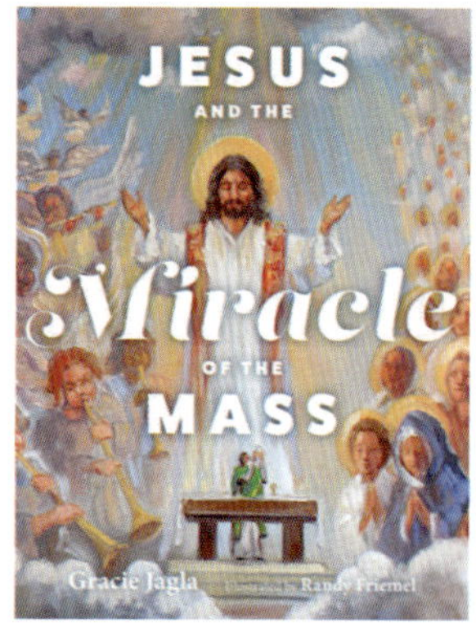

With beautiful illustrations and memorable rhyme, this book introduces children to the miracle that occurs at every Mass — the bread and wine on the altar transformed into the real presence of Jesus. Told from the unique and intimate perspective of Jesus himself, the story explains the incredible gift that the Eucharist is for us.

Saintly Rhymes Through the Year
by Meghan Bausch

Five years after perennial favorite ***Saintly Rhymes for Modern Times*** was first published, author and illustrator Meghan Bausch is back with ***Saintly Rhymes Through the Year***. This all-new treasury highlights multiple saints per month with colorful illustrations and catchy rhymes, teaching children that everyone is called to be a saint!

Jesus, Were You Little?
by Sally Metzger

In ***Jesus, Were You Little?*** children full of questions and wonder take readers on a journey of discovery, making Jesus real and relatable to young and old. With innocent curiosity, children ask the King of kings if he ever climbed a tree, spilled his milk, or skinned his knee.

Visit osvkids.com/books for more

Meet Sister Mary Margaret
by Rebecca W. Martin

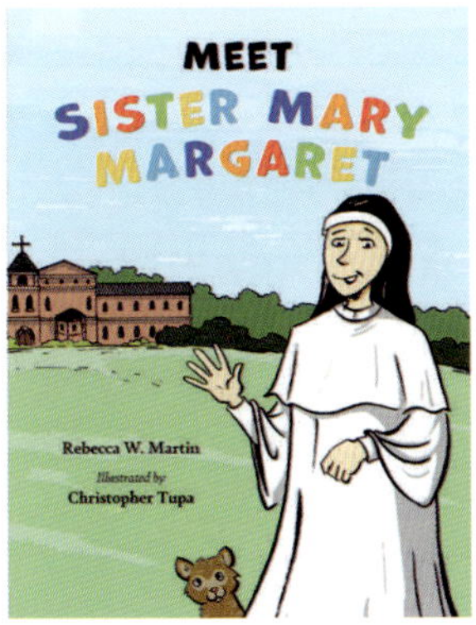

Meet Sister Mary Margaret answers the questions that children (but really, everyone!) have when first encountering a religious sister: "Why do you wear that?"; "What do you do all day?"; and more. This engaging, informative book with playful illustrations will bring children and families to an awareness of the beautiful role of women religious in the Church and the world.

Go and Fear Nothing
by Patrick O'Hearn

Go and Fear Nothing brings to life for young people this incredible real-life story and Our Lady's message of praying for the conversion of sinners, learning our Catechism, receiving the Sacraments with devotion, and relying on her unfailing help. When we doubt ourselves or make excuses for our weaknesses, we can remember Our Lady's words to Adele: "Go and fear nothing. I will help you."

Arthur the Clumsy Altar Server
by Theresa Kiser

In this endearing children's story filled with charming illustrations, Arthur demonstrates perseverance, humility, and an unquenchable love of the Lord in pursuing his dream. Children will learn from Arthur that what matters most is the sincere desire to serve God - not performing perfectly.

Arthur the Clumsy Altar Server Rings the Bells by Theresa Kiser

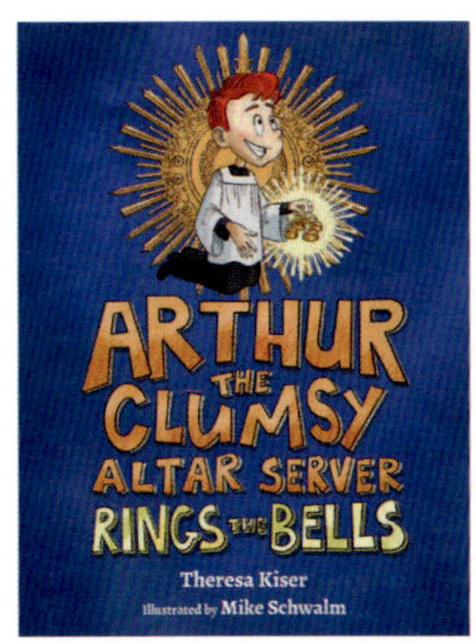

Find out what happens in the second installment of the Arthur the Clumsy Altar Server series. Through this endearing story, Arthur and readers alike will grow in understanding of the Blessed Sacrament and come to appreciate God's closeness to us in the Eucharist.

About the Author

Claudia Cangilla McAdam is an award-winning children's author with a master's degree in theology. She loves Sacred Scripture and has always wondered what it would be like to live in the time of Jesus. Many of her books invite children to enter into those Bible stories with her. Learn more about her at ClaudiaMcAdam.com.

About the Artist

Dave has been a freelance illustrator for 25 years and from his studio in Scotland has illustrated over 100 children's books as well as comic books, greeting cards, storyboards, and product packaging. He produces most of his work digitally although he still dabbles in traditional media and paints in oils and watercolor. Learn more about him at davehillsart.co.uk.